WELCOME TO OUR HOME.

Like a forest, this place grows richer with time—shaped by the people that pass through, the laughter that lingers, and the stories left behind.

We invite you to leave your mark in these pages. Share a memory from your stay, a note for future wanderers, a recipe from a shared meal, or a lesson whispered from the woods. Tell us what moved you, what surprised you, and what you'll carry with you when you journey home.

Because all that truly matters is here in the wild, waiting to be found.

POST
THIS SPACE FOR ADDRESS ONLY
ONE CENT STAMP HERE
LIFE
HAPPENS
OUTSIDE.

WHATEVER THE QUESTION, FRESH AIR IS THE ANSWER.

WE BELONG IN WILD PLACES.

When we slow down and notice the brightness of the stars, the patterns of a bird's song, and the changing sky, we get closer to what matters most.

WHEREVER YOU ROAM,

NATURE CALLS YOU HOME.

THE BEST ADVENTURES

ARE THE ONES WE

TAKE TOGETHER.

THIS IS A TIME TO GATHER—

FRIENDS AND FOOD, TREASURES AND TIME.

FOLLOW THE BREEZE, THE TRICKLE OF WATER,

AND THE WARMTH OF CONNECTION. FOLLOW THAT WHICH SUSTAINS.

EVERYTHING YOU NEED IS HERE,

AWAY FROM IT ALL.

RUSHING RIVERS MISS WHAT STILL WATERS REFLECT.

What was once a dream
has become a story—

captured in photographs,
maps, and mementos.

SEEK SHELTER,

FIND HOME.

SIMPLE DAYS BECOME BOUNTIFUL LIVES.

Linger a little longer—

when meals are shared,

when firelight dances,

and when the golden hour

gives way to twilight.

WHEN YOU FIND YOURSELF IN THE MOMENT, NOTHING IS LOST.

ALL WANDERERS ARE
WELCOME HERE.

REMEMBER WHERE
YOU CAME FROM,
WHAT BROUGHT YOU
HERE, AND WHAT
YOU'LL CARRY HOME.

THE DAYS WE SPEND CLOSE TO NATURE AND CLOSE TO EACH OTHER ARE THE DAYS THAT DEFINE OUR YEARS.

WHAT HAVE YOU NOTICED

THAT WASN'T THERE BEFORE?

THIS IS A PLACE WHERE LOST THINGS ARE FOUND, AND FOUND THINGS ARE CHERISHED.

THROUGH MEADOWS, THICKETS, AND MOUNTAIN RANGES—MAY EVERY TRAIL LEAD YOU HOME.

THERE IS NO GREATER GIFT

THAN THIS WILD LIFE.

Move with the sun,
follow the seasons,

and let nature
set the pace.

LEAVE NO TRACE EXCEPT A GOOD STORY.

HOME IS WHERE
EVERY CREATURE
FINDS COMFORT,
SAFETY, AND THE
FREEDOM TO BE.

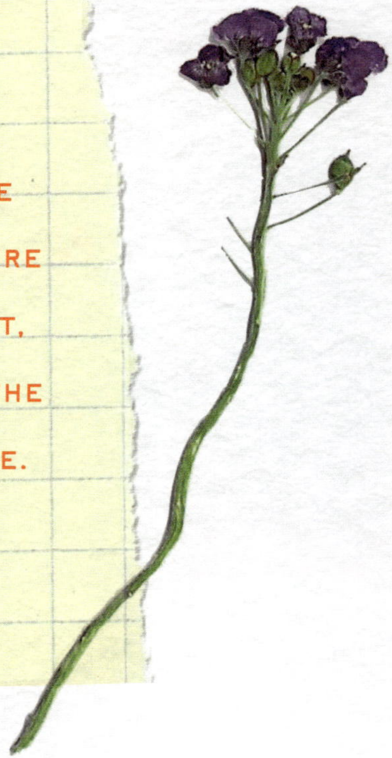

GOOD COMPANY MAKES FOR HAPPY TRAILS.

LIKE THE MEMORIES THAT CONNECT US,

HOMES ARE MEANT TO BE SHARED.

THE BEST STORIES
ARE TOLD OVER
CANDLELIGHT AND
CAMPFIRE.

YOU WERE HERE. THE LAND MAY NOT REMEMBER, BUT YOU WILL.

SOMETIMES WE NEED TO
TREK TO THE UNTAMED
EDGE OF THE WORLD
TO SEE THE BEAUTY OF
WHAT'S ALWAYS BEEN.

A SINGLE DAY AMONG THE TREES

CAN HOLD A LIFETIME OF ADVENTURE.

Travel reveals the fullness of life—when we realize our story is one of millions, unfolding all at once.

WHAT BEGAN AS A VISIT

BECAME SOMETHING LIKE HOME.

THIS PLACE IS TIMELESS—SO ARE YOUR MEMORIES.

WHEN IN DOUBT,
EXPLORE.

COMPENDIUM.
live inspired

An imprint of the Crown Publishing Group
A division of Penguin Random House LLC
1745 Broadway, New York, NY 10019
live-inspired.com | penguinrandomhouse.com

ISBN: 978-1-966077-08-4

Writer: Danielle Leduc McQueen
Designer: Caytlyn Cole Tolliver
Editor: Bailey Vega
Production Manager: Shannon Lery

Photography Credits:
Front cover, pages 6, 9, 14, 17, 21, 25, 29, 30, 34, 37, 41, 42, 45, 46, 49, 57, 58, 62, 65, 66, 70: Annie Spratt / unsplash.com; pages 5, 10, 13, 18, 22, 26, 30, 34, 37, 38, 41, 42, 50, 53, 54, 57, 61, 62, 65, 66, 73: Caytlyn Cole Tolliver.

1st printing. Manufactured in China with soy inks on FSC®-Mix certified paper.

The authorized representative in the EU for product safety and compliance is Penguin Random House Ireland, Morrison Chambers, 32 Nassau Street, Dublin D02 YH68, Ireland, https://eu-contact.penguin.ie.

Create meaningful moments with gifts that inspire.

CONNECT WITH US
live-inspired.com | sayhello@compendiuminc.com

@compendiumliveinspired
#compendiumliveinspired